MW01222228

To my dear
niece, Chris

Thanks for all
your help with
Ruth's book.

Jack & Ruth
Downs.

This book celebrates the 25th anniversary production of the stage play, *The Belle of Amherst* by William Luce.

The cover photograph by Gary Gabler was taken on September 10th, 2000. This photograph shows Julie Harris as Emily Dickinson, writing her poetry.

The Life of Emily Dickinson

By Douglas Westfall

Photographs of

JulieHarris as Emily Dickinson

from the Play
The Belle of Amherst
by William Luce

And Poetry by Emily

The Life of Emily Dickinson

Westfall, Douglas Paul, 1949—

Published by
The Paragon Agency
Orange, California, 2000

1. Julie Harris as Emily Dickinson
2. Dickinson, Emily, 1830-1886
3. History, poetry

I. Title.

ISBN: 1–891030-22-1

The Paragon Agency • Publishers
Photographs by Gary Gabler

First Printing • 1k • r1
Printed in USA

Contents

Acknowledgment vi

Dedication vii

Preface viii

Foreword ix

Playbill from the *Laguna Playhouse* xi

The Life of Emily Dickinson 1

Photographs of Julie Harris as Emily Dickinson and

    Poetry by Emily 31

Act I 33

Act II 79

List of First Lines of Poetry 120

Bibliography 121

Colophon 122

Acknowledgments

*Without the following people, this publication
would not have been possible.*

Julie Harris
William Luce
Linda L. Rowlett, Ph.D.
Kathleen Gunton

Charles Nelson Reilly
Don Gregory
Timothy Helgeson
Richard Stein

Andrew Barnicle
James Noone
Ken Billington
Alice Harkins
Lee Proudy
Gary Gabler

Reprinted by permission of the publishers and the Trustees of Amherst College from THE POEMS OF EMILY DICKINSON, Thomas H. Johnson, ed., Cambridge, Mass.: The Belknap Press of Harvard University Press, Copyright© 1951, 1955, 1979 by the President and Fellows of Harvard Collage.

The Publisher wishes to acknowledge the cooperation of

Richard Stein

for his help in producing this anniversary book and
for his permission and access to the

Laguna Playhouse

Laguna Beach, California
(949) 497-2787
www.LagunaPlayhouse.com

Dedication

This publication is lovingly dedicated to

Julie Harris

Preface

On September 7th, 2000, my wife and I went to the play *The Belle of Amherst*, at the **Laguna Playhouse** in Laguna Beach, California. This was our anniversary and it had been nearly a quarter of a century since I had seen the original.

We soon discovered we were sitting in front of William Luce, the author. Meeting with him the next day, we suggested our idea of this publication. Attending the play again that night, we also met with Julie Harris, Charles Nelson Reilly, Timothy Helgeson and Don Gregory.

As publishers, we approached the company with the idea of a 25th Anniversary book, celebrating the current production run of *The Belle of Amherst*. They were pleased.

We contacted our good friend and photographer, Gary Gabler and returned to the Laguna Playhouse again on Sunday, to photograph Julie during the play. Then we researched the life of Emily Dickinson, and with the help of Kathleen Gunton and Linda L. Rowlett, Ph.D., wrote this book.

Finally, we contacted *Harvard University Press* on Emily's poetry and *Samuel French, Inc.* on William Luce's play, and received permission to publish.

In 1975, William Luce, Charles Nelson Reilly and Timothy Helgeson collaborated on a one-woman play about Emily Dickinson for Julie Harris, the great stage actress. The following February, *The Belle of Amherst* opened in Seattle, Washington and proceeded to Broadway, New York.

Opening again, almost 25 years later, this lady and these three gentlemen, have brought back a reprise of *The Belle of Amherst*. Beginning in September, 2000 with the opening at the Laguna Playhouse in California, this new tour is sweeping the country. By April at the close of the tour, this will indeed be a quarter of a century in the making.

This has been a most rewarding experience.

We thank you all.

Douglas & Jackie Westfall

Foreword

THE EVERGREEN OF EMILY

by William Luce

The Belle of Amherst was my first foray into theater - written in 1975, a Broadway success in 1976. I little dreamed of the global life it would have. Now, twenty-five years later, *Belle* has been translated into many languages, with productions all over the world: England, Japan, Sweden, Australia, Brazil, Spain, Saudi Arabia, Iceland, France, Argentina, Russia, Norway, Mexico, South Africa, Italy, Israel, Denmark, Romania, Ireland, Singapore, Finland, Germany. It's as Julie Harris once observed: "We're riding a magic carpet."

The re-visiting of Emily's beloved Homestead through Miss Harris's anniversary tour is for me a return to creative essentials. I honed my craft of imagination through working with Miss Harris and director Charles Nelson Reilly. These unique friends inclined me in a strong direction, and since then, the soul of Emily Dickinson has been my touchstone.

Four years after Emily Dickinson's death in 1886, the first book of her poems was published. It was a modest volume, followed by two more in 1891 and 1896. After a piecemeal pattern of publication, the first complete collection of her poetry appeared in 1955. In like manner, Emily's correspondence was gathered and published. By similar process of increments, the miracle of Emily's mind and heart are still being revealed – in books, on television, on stage, in the concert hall. These hundred years following that first small collection of poems have seen the flowering of universal awareness, as if in compliance with her own words:

> I gained it so –
> By Climbing slow –
> By Catching at the Twigs that grow
> Between the Bliss – and me –

RICHARD STEIN
Executive Director

ANDREW BARNICLE
Artistic Director

By Special Arrangement with DON GREGORY

Present

JULIE HARRIS

in

The Belle of Amherst

A Play by

WILLIAM LUCE

Based on the life of Emily Dickinson

Compiled by

TIMOTHY HELGESON

Scenic Design by
JAMES NOONE

Lighting Design by
KEN BILLINGTON

Production Stage Manager
ALICE HARKINS

Directed by
CHARLES NELSON REILLY

The Life of Emily Dickinson

Emily Dickinson lived and died at the house in which she was born in Amherst, Massachusetts. Built by her grandfather, Samuel Dickinson, in 1813, the house was always called 'The Homestead'. It remains today, a large brick residence on Main Street – the first in Amherst. Emily was born there on December 10, 1830.

Due to a family financial crisis, The Homestead was sold in 1834 and Samuel moved to Ohio. Edward Dickinson, Emily's father, was the oldest of nine and determined he should restore the family's fortune. Edward bought half of the house and having a wife and three children to care for, he took over his father's law firm.

The family stayed in their part of the home until 1840 and moved to North Pleasant Street, selling the remainder of The Homestead to the other owner, Deacon David Mack. Emily was almost ten, and they stayed on Pleasant Street for 15 years. In late 1855, Edward repurchased The Homestead, moving his family back to his father's house. Emily lived there for the remainder of her life. The Homestead is shown (on page 4) on the map of early 1855 as *Mrs. D. Mack*.

Emily Dickinson is one of the most gifted poets in American literature. Since 1850, Emily wrote poetry for the remainder of her life. So prolific, between 1858 and 1865 she wrote over a thousand poems. Ordered to stop writing in 1865 by an eye doctor, she slowed the writing of her poetry to less than 50 a year, a pace that would decrease until her death. In June of 1884, she was stricken with Bright's disease, a kidney infection, and died two years later at age 55. Only two poems have been attributed to that last year.

The form of Emily's poetry was new. So new, that she was not recognized as an accomplished poet until years after her death. Of this, her mentor, the Reverend Thomas Wentworth Higginson of the <u>Atlantic Monthly</u> magazine, said:

> "The impression of a wholly new and original poetic genius was...distinct on my mind at the first reading...what place ought to be assigned in literature to what is so remarkable, yet so elusive..."

Emily corresponded with him throughout her life, perhaps partly in an effort to get him to publish her poems. She would never meet with success and Higginson would only help to publish her work after her death.

Until she began to write in earnest in 1858, she wrote less than one poem each year, with her first known poem in 1850. Few of her poems have titles and all are now referred to by their first lines.

All the poems included here are complete and unedited as Emily wrote them and can be found by a reference number, eg: (J108), in Thomas H. Johnson's epic work, <u>The Complete Poems of Emily Dickinson</u>, 1957, Little, Brown & Company.

Amherst in 1855 was largely a collection of farms, each with its own barn and outhouse. The population hovered under 3,000, including the East Village and surrounding area. Main Street ran east and west, Pleasant Street went north and south, with the Commons south of Main.

South Pleasant became Broadway at the Commons and southeast from there, was Amherst College. The Amherst and Belchertown Railroad was well east of the Commons; the cemetery, on North Pleasant.

Always a source for literary genius, Amherst was the home to many famous authors, poets and even a famous librarian. *Melvin Dewey* was at the Amherst College Library in the 1870s, across from the college, when he developed the Dewey Decimal System. *Noah Webster* started work on his <u>Dictionary of the American Language</u> during the 1810s when he lived near the center of town. Much later, the poet *Robert Frost* lived here in the 1920s and '30s.

Emily Elizabeth Dickinson was named for her mother Emily and her father's sister *Elisabeth;* Lavinia for their mother's sister, Lavinia Norcross. Her brother, William Austin, was named for her father's brother, William. Austin was older than Emily

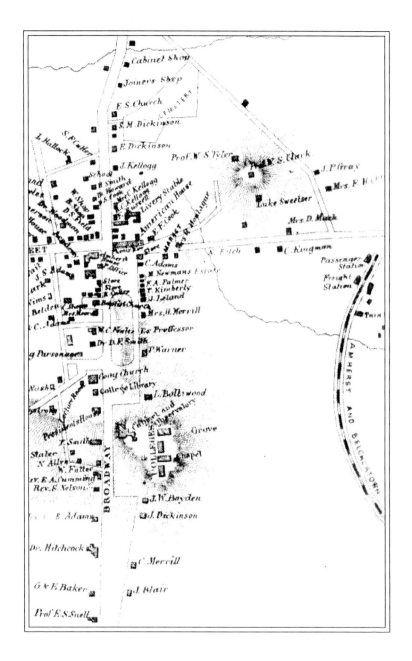

[Map of Amherst, 1855 - Population 2,937]

by a year and Lavinia, younger by three.

The Dickinsons had been in Hampshire County since 1659, and many members of Emily's family lived in Amherst. There are several Dickinsons on the map of 1855 and one sister of Emily's father, Caroline, married a local, Joseph Sweetser. Joseph's brother Luke had a general store in town and later helped start the Amherst and Belchertown Railroad. Deacon Luke Sweetser, who lived just north of The Homestead, was the uncle of Abby Wood, a school friend of Emily's.

In 1837, the Nelson sisters started a primary school in their home, south of the Common and across the street from Amherst College. There, Emily met many of her early friends. One friendship with Abiah Root began in 1844 that continued through letters after Abiah moved away. Another friend, Emeline Kellogg, lived just south of Emily on Pleasant Street. Emeline's father James had the Joiners Shop, just north of the cemetery and was nationally renowned for his woodwork. Still another, Emily Fowler, was a friend whose grandfather was Noah Webster.

Lavinia too had friends. Jennie Hitchcock was the daughter of the Reverend Doctor Edward Hitchcock - president of Amherst College. The Hitchcocks lived south of the college, across the street. Later, Jennie was Lavinia's roommate at Ipswitch Female Seminary.

Emily's family, at that time, lived next to the cemetery on North Pleasant Street until late 1855. The family had needed more room and so her father bought the home on Pleasant Street.

The Pleasant Street house was a wood frame structure and had a garden at the back. There was an apple orchard behind that and beyond, a grove of white pines - all planted by her father. Austin tended the orchard and Emily, the garden. With neighbors to the north and south however, the Pleasant Street home did not have the open feeling of The Homestead.

Emily at age ten went to Amherst Academy (founded by her grandfather Samuel,) after attending four years of primary school, as did Lavinia. Both girls had a normal upbringing with dances and school to occupy their time. Austin went to Williston Seminary and later Amherst College, also founded by their grandfather.

One interesting individual, Sylvester Graham, also attended Amherst Academy. Known later as a health food fanatic, the graham cracker is named for him.

By age 17, Emily had spent a year at Mount Holyoke Female Seminary, founded by Mary Lyon. Miss Lyon grew up in Amherst attending Amherst Academy as well, years before Emily. In 1836, Miss Lyon started her school in South Hadley nearby, where she died in 1849 - the year after Emily left. It was during Emily's time at Mount Holyoke that her only photograph was taken, a daguerreotype.

A daguerreotype (1840-1860s) is the best known kind of early photographic processes. A positive image is usually found with a matt-mask between the actual photographic plate and the surface glass. A paper or cloth seal around the edges, holds the pieces together.

Louis J. M. Daguerre, a French Basque, began working with photography during 1829 in France. Not until 1838 did he discover by accident, the process which bears his name. Samuel F. B. Morse, the inventor of the telegraph, was the first American to see a daguerreotype, in 1839. He then brought the photographic process to America, setting up a studio in New York.

Although Emily had a good start on her education, she left school with anxiety about the efforts to coerce her into 'standing up to be a Christian.' Unable to make her professions of faith, she left the school after nine months. Her father said it was homesickness that brought her permanently back home from Mount Holyoke.

Emily, in her younger years, dressed in the convention of the day, at least for a young girl in her teens. Later in life she dressed only in white, much to the curiosity of the town, and did so year round. Normally, fashion dictated that darker colors were to be worn from Autumn through Winter.

> Fashions prevailed in the 1850s, '60s and '70s, through magazines such as *Harper's Weekly* published in NY, *Harper's Bazar* also NY, and *Godey's Lady's Book and Magazine*, published out of Philadelphia.

It was not uncommon in mid-19th century New England, for women to stay at their father's home and not marry, especially those of affluent families. Neither Emily or Lavinia ever married.

One event that came to Amherst brightened

Emily's life. Welch's National Circus came to Amherst in 1852 with the profound announcement in the local newspaper: *"...the entree into this town will be of a grandeur beggaring description..."* Twenty-five years later she wrote to Mrs. Holland (wife of the editor to the <u>Springfield Republican</u>) after another: "A circus passed the house – still I feel the red in my mind though the drums are out."

Many of Emily's friends and childhood acquaintances died at young age and were reflected in her poetry. Five alone perished from tuberculosis (consumption) while she lived on Pleasant Street. Martha and Sarah Humphrey both died of the disease - in 1851 (age 20) and 1854 (age 18) - respectively. Their sister Jane had been a classmate of Emily's at Mount Holyoke.

Her close friend Benjamin F. Newton read law at her father's office in Amherst and gave Emily a book of Ralph Waldo Emerson's poems in 1850. Benjamin died only three years later at age 32. Emily wrote this to Higginson:

"When a little girl, I had a friend who taught me Immortality; but venturing too near, himself, he never returned."

There is a continued presence of death in Emily's poetry for death was always present in Emily's life and in Amherst – as shown in the following poems:

She died — this was the way she died. (J150)
I reason, Earth is short — (J301)
Because I could not stop for Death — (J712)
Regularly on Sunday afternoons, the townspeople

brought flowers to the cemetery, passing Emily's home. In fact, the death rate of young people in Amherst is startling. Here under age 25 are all those who died from 1851 through 1854. They were buried in the cemetery while Emily lived next door:

Amherst Burials Under 25

1851	February 5th	Betsey Packard	19
	March 3rd	Fanny Field	23
	April 19th	Abby Ann Haskell	19
	June 23rd	James Francis Billings	20
	July 17th	Ellen Russell	19
	October 27th	Jane Ballou Grout	19
	October 30th	Martha Kingman	19
	November 15th	Ellen Kingman	13
	December 17th	Emeline Packard	24
1852	March 26th	Ellen Stanley	18
	June 7th	Catherine Woolsey	8
	November 28th	Jane Thayer	21
1853	January 9th	Charles Converse	18
	April 20th	Anna Charlotte Warner	11
	August 15th	Enos Perry	20
	October 10th	Charles Morton Howland	22
	October 30th	Sarah Church	22
	December 2nd	Ann Augusta Hutchinson	21
	December 5th	Franklin Ebenezer Hawley	21
	December 20	Frederick Warren Lane	23
	December 29	William Boerhaave Gooch	19
1854	March 14	Sarah Field	17
	May 19	Dwight Cowan	23
	May 26	Jane Juliette Kingman	31

(Jane Kingman at age 31 is mentioned here as the third and last daughter of Colonel Cyrus Kingman to die within three years.)

Emily began to write poetry as valentines. Her first published piece was indeed a valentine, but not a poem. It was published in the Amherst College student publication.

1850 <u>The Amherst College Indicator</u>

Magnum bonum

"Magnum bonum, "harum scarum," zounds et zounds, et war alarum, man reformam, life perfectum, mundum changum, all things flarum?

Sir, I desire an interview; meet me at sunrise, or sunset, or the new moon - the place is immaterial. In gold, or in purple, or sackcloth - I look not upon the raiment..."

The first known poem written by Emily Dickinson was sent during Valentine's week – as a valentine – in 1850 to Elbridge Bowdoin, her father's law partner. He was ten years older than Emily. Emily often met the men in her father's business life and those in Austin's. In later years, the poet Ralph Waldo Emerson, who preferred to be called Waldo, visited Austin and Sue's home. Emily however, was not invited.

In 1854, Deacon Mack died and The Homestead went up for sale the following year. The Homestead was then repurchased by Edward. At that time, the Dickinson family was prosperous.

The Dickinsons were well educated. Samuel, Emily's grandfather, graduated from Dartmouth Law School and helped found both Amherst Academy and Amherst College. Edward had attended Yale and Austin went to Williston Seminary, Amherst College and Harvard Law School. Both Samuel and Edward were called 'Squire' because of their law degrees. Emily's mother Emily had attended a boarding school in Connecticut.

Samuel, Edward and Austin, three generations of Dickinsons, then attended three of the big four colleges:

> By the 1800s, Harvard, Yale, Princeton and Dartmouth were considered the big four: the most significant and prominant colleges in America. Later, Columbia, Brown, Cornell and the University of Pennsylvania were then added to the 'League,' making eight. But the 'Four League Schools,' or *IV League* at the time, were considered the choice schools of higher education.

Both Edward and Austin served as treasurer at Amherst College and later Edward became a state representative and was subsequently a member of Congress. Both Emily and Lavinia had a sound education, attending the Nelson's primary school and Amherst Academy. Emily then went to Mount Holyoke – although her schooling was cut short – and Lavinia, Ipswitch Seminary.

Although Emily's father was considered dispassionate, the story is true of his younger years when he rang the bells in the church to tell others of the beautiful sunset. He seemed to save his passion for church. The family was religious, as wrote Emily to Higginson:

> "They are religious, except me, and address an eclipse, every morning, whom they call their 'Father.'"

Edward, his wife Emily and daughter Lavinia joined the First Congregational Church in 1850, and Emily did not. Eventually Emily stopped going to church altogether. See the poem:

Some keep the Sabbath going to Church - (J324)

Emily's reluctance to attend church or follow a formal religion did not however, deter her from a strong belief in God. She had read only the Bible up until Austin, as a boy, began to sneak literature into the home and hide it in the piano.

Edward Dickinson was known as an austere if not demanding man. His photograph of 1853, shows nothing different. His strict behavior was a requirement in his life. Amherst College had been near bankruptcy and The Homestead sold off. Taking over his father's firm in 1834and the Amherst College treasury at the same time, was part of his resolve to right both the college and his own birthright.

He was the quintessential patriarch of the family. Firm and stoic, he believed strongly that *"Honesty is the best policy,"* as he wrote to his son and eventual law partner, Austin.

Previous to studying law, Austin had taught school

in Boston. Emily visited Austin there only once. She preferred, as did her father, to have Austin in Amherst. After finishing law school at Harvard, Austin lived in Amherst for the remainder of his days – as was his father's wish.

What allowed Edward to succeed, even during a national depression, was his firm temperament. He showed the same face to everyone, except perhaps Emily, his daughter. She was perhaps his brightest light. Her father may have never read her work, but he was well aware of her poetry.

Emily's father Edward fought for the Amherst and Belchertown Railroad to come to Amherst, which it did in 1853 – all nineteen and a half miles of it. This made it easier for him to reach Boston where he was in the State Legislature and later a Congressman.

With the family back in The Homestead and Austin returned from law school, life began to be more secure for Emily. Austin married Susan Gilbert, Emily's childhood friend, the following year. Emily's father built a home for them, The Evergreens, just west of The Homestead in 1857. The relationship between Emily and Sue, for the time, grew.

The Homestead, built by Samuel Dickinson, is an imposing edifice. The two story brick home had no less that nine rooms when Edward added a two story back wing in 1855 to include a kitchen and washroom. Somewhat out of town on Main Street, The Homestead had gardens and an orchard like the house on Pleasant Street; however, there was not another building within several hundred feet. The only exception was Colonel Cyrus Kingman's place, across the street from where The Evergreens would soon be built.

Two major social events in Amherst were the Commencement services at Amherst College in August - in which the Dickinsons always participated - and the annual Cattle Show in October. One year Emily's Indian bread won second prize at the show - her baking was renowned.

Emily was well known in town for her baking and her garden. Her famous 'Black Cake' recipe – with 19 eggs – has been handed down and transcribed into a reduced form:

BLACK CAKE RECIPE
by Emily Dickinson

2 cups sifted flour
2 cups sugar
½ pound butter
5 eggs
1 pound raisins
$^2/_3$ pound currants
$^2/_3$ pound citron
¼ - ½ cup brandy
¼ cup molasses
½ nutmeg, ground
1 teaspoon cloves
1 teaspoon mace
1 teaspoon cinnamon
½ teaspoon baking soda
½ teaspoon of salt -
     (if unsalted butter is used)

Add sugar gradually to butter. Blend until light and creamy. Add unbeaten eggs and molasses. Beat well. Re-sift flour with baking soda and spices. Beat sifted ingredients into mixture, alternating with brandy.

Stir in raisins, currants, and citron. Pour batter into two loaf pans lined with waxed paper. Place a shallow pan of water in bottom of oven below pans. Bake in cake pans in a moderately hot oven (225 degrees) for <u>three hours</u>. Remove water pan for last half hour - make sure water does not evaporate.

Let cool. Remove waxed paper; wrap in fresh paper - some say kitchen parchment. It tastes best if it is stored in a cool, dry place for several hours, overnight or even for days. Emily kept hers in the cellar over a month before eating, as some people do still today.

There were two newspapers available to the Dickinson household, <u>The Springfield Republican</u> – a daily and the <u>Hampshire and Franklin Express</u>, published each Friday. Such drastic tales as follows were given to entertain the country town folk:

"A young woman, using a window to enter her house, was caught by the falling sash and was 'perfectly dead' when discovered."

"A young lady was caught by the hair in a revolving shaft in Chelmsford Mills and scalped."

Emily wrote about them to Dr. Holland, a later editor of the <u>Springfield Republican</u>: "Who writes those funny accidents...?" But, she would read them to Lavinia, in the early evening.

Emily's immediate family, brother Austin, sister Lavinia, and their parents, Edward and Emily Dickinson, remained close to each other all their lives. Other than schooling and several visits out of town, they lived close to each other until each of their deaths. With Austin's moving next door after marriage to Susan Huntington Gilbert, the family stayed together from then on.

Emily continued to retreat from society - with her friends gone, her family dying off and her relationships fading. She never went out, never to anyone's home and after 1865 – the year of her eye problem – never again left Amherst. Her mother too had begun, back in 1855, a long illness that would continue to erode her health. Emily and Lavinia took care of her.

Although Emily is known for her poetry, with many poems sent as valentines, she also sent letters with 'epigrams' - one-line thoughts of deep and probing wisdom. Here are three:

> *Hereafter, I will pick no Rose,*
> *lest it fade or prick me.*

> *The sailor cannot see the North –*
> *but knows the Needle can–*

> *We must be careful what we say.*
> *No bird resumes its egg.*

Emily's poetry – one or two written as early as 1850 – started to develop by 1858, during which she wrote over 50 poems. Her poems have been dated by the handwriting and dates on letters in which she included her work. Many poems by Emily Dickinson, up to 120, are not datable.

Emily long had thought of herself as a poet although the few poems published within her lifetime - no more than ten - were all published anonymously. None was ever published under her own name until four years after her death.

Most of Emily's earlier published works may have been published through the help of Samuel Bowles, Editor of <u>The Springfield Republican</u>, the newspaper her father read. Following are some of Emily's poems published while she was living:

> 1852   **<u>The Springfield Republican</u>,**
> *"Sic transit gloria manta,"* (J3)
> 1861   **<u>The Springfield Republican</u>,**
> *I taste a liquor never brewed* (J214)
> 1862   **<u>The Springfield Republican</u>,**
> *Safe in their Alabaster Chambers* (J216)
> 1864   **<u>Round Table</u>,**
> *Some keep the Sabbath going to Church* (J324)
> 1866   **<u>The Springfield Republican</u>,**
> *A narrow Fellow in the Grass* (J986)

[See the poetyr index at the back of the book.]

In April of 1862, an article in the *Atlantic Monthly* magazine entitled "Letter to a Young Contributor" prompted Emily Dickinson to send four poems to

Thomas Wentworth Higginson, the author. She was then 31. Higginson wrote back requesting more and just over a week later, Emily sent three.

At this point in her life, she had written well over 300 poems and by the end of that year would more than double the number. Six weeks later she sent another letter and for the remainder of her life thought of herself as Higginson's 'scholar' and he her 'preceptor' although he would never himself publish her poetry.

Of her letters, Thomas Wentworth Higginson wrote in 1891:

"On April 16, 1862, I took from the post office in Worcester, Mass., where I was then living, the following letter: -

MR. HIGGINSON, - Are you too deeply occupied to say if my verse is alive? The mind is so near itself it cannot see distinctly, and I have none to ask. Should you think it breathed, and had you the leisure to tell me, I should feel quick gratitude. If I make the mistake, that you dared to tell me would give me sincerer honor toward you. I inclose my name, asking you, if you please, sir, to tell me what is true? That you will not betray me it is needless to ask, since honor is its own pawn.

The letter was postmarked Amherst."

The four poems she sent were:

Safe in their alabaster chambers (J216),
I'll tell you how the sun rose (J318),
We play at Paste (J320) and
The nearest dream recedes unrealized (J319).

The first two are published in this volume. The first was originally published anonymously in 1862; the second not until 1890. Letters to Higginson contained other poems including *A bird came down the walk* (J328).

Emily's second letter to Higginson and the three additional poems came ten days later. Higginson continues (excerpted):

"Her second letter (received April 26, 1862), was as follows: -

MR. HIGGINSON,--Your kindness claimed earlier gratitude, but I was ill, and write to-day from my pillow.

Thank you for the surgery; it was not so painful as I supposed. I bring you others, as you ask, though they might not differ. While my thought is undressed, I can make the distinction; but when I put them in the gown, they look alike and numb.

You asked how old I was? I made no verse, but one or two, until this winter, sir.

You ask of my companions. Hills, sir, and the sundown, and a dog large as myself, that my father bought me. They are better than beings because they know, but do not tell; and the noise in the pool at noon excels my piano.

But I fear my story fatigues you. I would like to learn. Could you tell me how to grow, or is it unconveyed, like melody or witchcraft?

I could not weigh myself. My size felt small to me. I read your chapters in the Atlantic, and experienced honor for you. I was sure you would not reject a confiding question.

Is this, sir, what you asked me to tell you? Your friend,

E. DICKINSON."

Emily's "dog large as myself" was a gift from her father sometime in the 1860s. She named him Carlo. Much later, Higginson received this note:

"AMHERST.

Carlo died.

E. DICKINSON.

Would you instruct me now?"

The three poems she sent with the second letter are:

South Winds jostle them (J86);
Of all the Sounds despatched abroad (J321); and
There came a Day at Summer's full (J322).

She also sent him a third letter but this one came with

the realization that he would never publish her work. Higginson goes on (excerpted):

"This was received June 8, 1862.

DEAR FRIEND,--Your letter gave no drunkenness, because I tasted rum before. Domingo comes but once; yet I have had few pleasures so deep as your opinion, and if I tried to thank you, my tears would block my tongue.

If fame belonged to me, I could not escape her; if she did not, the longest day would pass me on the chase, and the approbation of my dog would forsake me then. My barefoot rank is better.

The sailor cannot see the North, but knows the needle can.

But, will you be my preceptor, Mr. Higginson?"

Higginson later says,

"I must soon have written to ask her for her picture, To this came the following reply, in July, 1862:-

Could you believe me without? I had no portrait, now, but am small, like the wren; and my hair is bold, like the chestnut bur; and my eyes, like the sherry in the glass, that the guest leaves. Would this do just as well?"

Thomas Higginson visited her only twice, once in

1870 and later, wrote this about this visit in 1891:

"She came toward me with two day-lilies, which she put in a childlike way into my hand, saying softly, under her breath, 'These are my introduction,' and adding, also, under her breath, in childlike fashion, 'Forgive me if I am frightened; I never see strangers, and hardly know what I say.'"

Higginson's first visit with Emily left her with a feeling of loss. She knew she would never be published and although he would still receive her poems, they would go no further. This stayed true through the end of her life.

The people in Emily's life took on a greater importance as she withdrew from her society. Thomas Higginson, wrote about the "...recluse character of her life..." but only years after her death.

In 1860, her Aunt Lavinia died. She was Emily's mother's sister and although not close by, her death had an effect on Emily as those around her diminished in number. She relied more and more on her immediate family - her mother and sister Lavinia - for company.

Youthful in nature, Emily perhaps never really wanted to grow up. Her isolation was only from adults, not children. She baked gingerbread for them and played their games, only to run off if another adult came to her door.

Her father was away much of the time as was her

brother Austin. Austin's wife Sue became again closer to Emily after they had moved to The Evergreens, next door. Emily wrote to Higginson:

"I have a brother and sister; my mother does not care for thought, and father, too busy with his briefs to notice what we do."

On a trip to Boston, in June of 1874, Emily's father Edward died of a heart attack. She was heartbroken. With her pace of writing already decreasing, it now slowed more. Her father, although never considered a warm man, represented the strength of her family and she idolized him. Exactly one year and a day from that event, her mother suffered a stroke and was paralyzed for the rest of her life.

In a brief note to Higginson, she wrote:

"DEAR FRIEND,--Mother was paralyzed Tuesday, a year from the evening father died. I thought perhaps you would care.
YOUR SCHOLAR."

Emily is considered the most gifted female poet in American Literature and today is compared with poets like Walt Whitman. Classical Literature and popular American writers were prevalent in Emily's life, as she wrote to Higginson in 1862:

"For poets, I have Keats, and Mr. and Mrs. Browning. For prose, Mr. Ruskin, Sir Thomas Browne, and the Revelations. Father...buys me many books, but begs me not to read them, because he fears they joggle the mind."

Through her brother Austin, Emily knew Ralph Waldo Emerson and Emily became exposed to literature through her friend Helen Hunt Jackson. Helen, who although had lived in Colorado and California, grew up and was buried in Amherst.

Helen lived just south of the Nelson sisters on Broadway and also had attended Amherst Academy. Helen encouraged Emily about her poetry and tried to get Emily to publish her work later in her life, to no avail, Emily eventually gave up on ever being a published poet. Helen is buried in the West Cemetery as are Emily and most of Emily's family.

A poem possibly written in 1859 was published anonymously in 1878, probably with the help of her friend Helen. Helen Hunt Jackson wrote *Ramona*, a historical novel about Native Americans, set in early California. Helen is credited for at least this anonymous publication of Emily's work:

1878 **A Mask of Poets**
Success is counted sweetest (J67)

Yet, Emily continued to strive in her work, although the volume of poetry in numbers was greatly reduced. She perhaps wrote less than 25 poems in 1878.

Emily had some relationship with at least two individuals: Reverend Charles Wadsworth and Judge Otis Phillips Lord. Emily had met Reverand

Wadsworth in the 1850s, she saw him first at his Presbyterian church in Philadelphia.

She was so impressed by Wadsworth, it is thought that her 'Master' letters were written were to him. Emily also wrote of her purported love. If Wadsworth (who was married) was her Master, then his visit becomes even more defining. It was their last time together – he died in 1883.

Millicent Todd Bingham's book in 1954, <u>Emily Dickinson - A Revelation</u>, shows Emily's relationship with Judge Lord. Although he was 18 years her senior, his wife had died years before. Still, the answer to the mystery of Emily's writings of romance eludes everyone.

A fire on July 4, 1879, destroyed most of the Merchants Row on South Pleasant Street. Wrote Amherst College Professor, William S. Tyler:

> "Woke up to hear & see this morning that most of the business part of the town, hotel, Post Office, Savings Bank, book stores & principal shops had been burned out during the night."

It seems most of the town heard the bells but thought it was the July 4th celebration. Emily too, if she had seen it, would have only seen the fire from a distance at The Homestead.

In her younger years, Emily traveled. She had been to Boston, in 1844, 1846, 1851 and also 1864-65 when she saw the eye specialist Dr. Henry Williams.

She had gone to Washington DC in 1854 and Philadelphia on the same trip and she had been to Springfield and even Connecticut. Her greatest travels were in her poetry. See:

I never saw a Moor – (J1052)

Emily, though she never left her father's house for the last twenty years of her life, traveled through her mind.

In 1883, her last year of good health, Emily and her younger sister Lavinia lived alone at The Homestead, caring for each other with the help of their maid-servant, Maggie Maher. Emily's mother had been paralyzed the last seven years of her life and died in 1882 and Emily's writing of poetry slowed again. Sue now came over infrequently but Austin helped take care of his sisters.

Maggie Maher lived south of the railroad tracks and although she stayed the night at The Homestead, she left for her own home every afternoon. Maggie had been with the family since the 1870s and would continue there until Lavinia's death in 1899.

The daguerreotype of Emily, mentioned before, has its own story. An albumen photographic copy was made from the original after Emily's death in order to illustrate a book of her published poems. Neither Austin nor Lavinia liked the picture and they tried in vain to alter its appearance by duplication. The daguerreotype had belonged to Maggie Maher maid and has never been found. This copy is now the only picture of Emily that exists.

Other people had begun to pass away from Emily's

life. Samuel Bowles, who had published her first few poems, died in 1881, Dr. Josiah Holland who took over *The Springfield Republican* and eventually started *Century Magazine* died in 1882. Reverend Wadsworth died in 1883 and Judge Lord in 1884.

Still, Austin's three children gave Emily company and joy, especially the youngest, little Gilbert. Little Gilbert's Aunt Emily was his favorite and they were very close. Tragically little Gilbert died at age eight from typhoid fever in 1883, the year after her mother's death. Nothing else in Emily's life saddened her more than little Gilbert's passing. She wrote this to Sue:

> *"They dropped like Flakes-, They dropped like Stars-, Like Petals from a Rose–…"*

Austin and Sue never got over it.

Two years after her mother's death, Emily had her first attack of Bright's disease. It would debilitate her and after two years, take her life. In spite of her illness, she still wrote poetry – eleven in 1885 with her last year bringing two. A week before her death, she slipped into unconsciousness and then was gone.

Emily had wanted a service in her own home and to be carried through the garden to the cemetery – so she would never lose sight of The Homestead. This was done for her. Excerpts of her obituary, written by Sue, Austin's wife, are as follows:

> "Very few in the village…knew Miss Emily personally, although the facts of her seclusion and her intellectual brilliancy were familiar

Amherst traditions."

"Her talk and her writings were like no one's else, and...So intimate and passionate was her love of Nature, she seemed herself a part of the high March sky, the summer day and bird-call."

"To her life was rich, and all aglow with God and immortality. With no creed, no formulate faith, ...she walked this life with the gentleness and reverence of old saints..."

published unsigned

In her life, Emily Dickinson wrote 1,775 poems. Yet, only perhaps ten were published before her death and all of those without her name. She sewed her poems into 'packets' and after Emily's death, Lavinia found 60 packets containing some 900 poems in a box and many others loose in a drawer.

One hundred fifteen poems were first published in 1890, with the help of Thomas Higginson, although he edited them. The following year, 166 more were published and in 1894 and additional 102. In 1896, 66 more with previous published verses came out in an edition. Fame had finally reached Emily, years after she was gone.

Emily wrote different versions of some poems. Also, there are a few unfinished works. The only complete publication of her works did not come out until the 1950s.

Shortly before Emily died, she sent a note to her cousins, Aunt Libby's children: Lavinia, Louisa and Frances. It read:

"Little Cousins, — Called back."

Emily somehow, seemed to know.

Emily Dickinson is a jewel in American literature. She once wrote:

> "Is it oblivion or absorption when things pass from our minds? Truth is such a rare thing, it is delightful to tell it. I find ecstacy in living; the mere sense of living is joy enough."

NOTE

All of the following poems are complete and have a date & number, eg: 1862/1890 — (J303). The first is the estimated year Emily wrote the poem, the second is the first year it was published and the number is the reference to the poems listed Johnson's book.

[See the poetry index at the back of the book.]

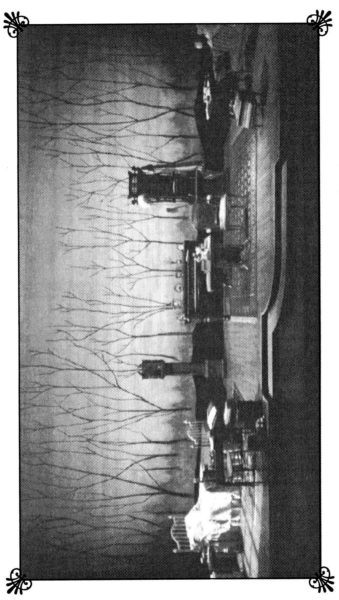

Stage set from the Laguna Playhouse production.

Selected Poems by
Emily Dickinson

Photographs of

JULIE HARRIS as

Emily Dickinson

Act I

This is my introduction...
Forgive me if I am frightened; I never see
strangers, and hardly know what I say.

The Soul selects her own Society —
Then — shuts the Door —
To her divine Majority —
Present no more —

Unmoved — she notes the Chariots — pausing —
At her low Gate —
Unmoved — an Emperor be kneeling
Upon her Mat —

I've known her — from an ample nation —
Choose One —
Then — close the Valves of her attention —
Like Stone —

1862c/1890 — (J303)

Her famous 'Black Cake' recipe has been handed down and transcribed – revived by The Belle of Amherst.

Stir in raisins, currants, and citron.
Bake in cake pans in a moderately hot oven
for <u>three hours</u>.

"We must be careful what we say.
No bird resumes its egg."

Surgeons must be very careful
When they take the knife!
Underneath their fine incisions
Stirs the Culprit — *Life!*

1859c/1891 — (J108)

Tell all the Truth but tell it slant —
Success in Circuit lies
Too bright for our infirm Delight
The Truth's superb surprise

As Lightning to the Children eased
With explanation kind
The Truth must dazzle gradually
Or every man be blind —

1868c/1945 — (J1129)

From 1850, Emily wrote poetry for the remainder of her life.

A word is dead
When it is said,
Some say.
I say it just
Begins to live
That day.

1872?/1894 — (J1212)

If I can stop one Heart from breaking
I shall not live in vain
If I can ease one Life the Aching
Or cool one Pain

Or help one fainting Robin
Unto his Nest again
I shall not live in Vain.

1864c/1890 — (J919)

*Emily began her poetry by sending them as
valentines and did so for the first few years.*

Awake ye muses nine, sing me a strain divine,
Unwind the solemn twine, and tie my Valentine!

Oh the Earth was *made* for lovers, for damsel, and hopeless
    swain,
For sighing, and gentle whispering, and *unity* and of *twain.*
All things do go a courting, in earth, or sea, or air,
God hath made nothing single but *thee* in His world so fair!
The *bride,* and then the *bridegroom,* the *two,* and then the
    one,
Adam, and Eve, his consort, the moon, and then the sun;
The life doth prove the precept, who obey shall happy be,
Who will not serve the sovereign, be hanged on fatal tree.
The high do seek the lowly, the great do seek the small,
None cannot find who *seeketh,* on this terrestrial ball;
The bee doth court the flower, the flower his suit receives,
And they make merry wedding, whose guests are hundred
    leaves;
The wind doth woo the branches, the branches they are won,
And the father fond demandeth the maiden for his son.
The storm doth walk the seashore humming a mournful tune,
The wave with eye so pensive, looketh to see the moon,
Their spirits meet together, they make them solemn vows,
No more he singeth mournful, her sadness she doth lose.

(cont.)

The first poem of Emily Dickinson was sent during Valentine's week – as a valentine – in 1850.

The *worm* doth woo the *mortal*, death claims a living bride,
Night unto day is married, morn unto eventide;
Earth is a merry damsel, and *heaven* a knight so true,
And Earth is quite coquettish, and beseemeth in vain to sue.
Now to the *application*, to the reading of the roll,
To bringing thee to justice, and marshalling thy soul:
Thou art a *human* solo, a being cold, and lone,
Wilt have no kind companion, thou *reap'st* what thou hast
    sown.
Hast never silent hours, and minutes all too long,
And a deal of sad reflection, and *wailing* instead of song?
There's *Sarah*, and *Eliza*, and *Emeline* so fair,
And *Harriet*, and *Susan*, and she with *curling hair*!
Thine eyes are sadly blinded, but yet thou mayest see
Six true, and comely maidens sitting upon the tree;
Approach that tree with caution, then up it boldly climb,
And seize the one thou lovest, nor care for *space*, or *time*!
Then bear her to the greenwood, and build for her a bower,
And give her what she asketh, jewel, or bird, or flower —
And bring the fife, and trumpet, and beat upon the drum —
And bid the world Goodmorrow, and go to glory home!

1850/1894 — (J1)

"*I find ecstacy in living; the mere sense
of living is joy enough.*"

I dwell in Possibility —
A fairer House than Prose —
More numerous of Windows —
Superior — for Doors —

Of Chambers as the Cedars —
Impregnable of Eye —
And for an Everlasting Roof
The Gambrels of the sky —

Of Visitors — the fairest —
For Occupation — This —
The spreading wide my narrow Hands
To gather Paradise —

1862c/1929 — (J657)

This Me — that walks and works — must die,
Some fair or stormy Day.
Adversity if it may be
Or wild prosperity
The Rumor's Gate was shut so tight
Before my mind was born
Not even a Prognostic's push
Can make a Dent thereon —

1883c/1945 — (J1588)

*The Nelson sisters started a primary school
in their home, south of the Common.*

Emily went to Mount Holyoke and Lavinia,
the Ipswitch Seminary.

*Many of Emily's friends and childhood acquaintances,
died at a young age.*

There's been a Death, in the Opposite House,
As lately as Today —
I know it, by the numb look
Such Houses have — alway —

The Neighbors rustle in and out —
The Doctor — drives away —
A Window opens like a Pod —
Abrupt — mechanically —

Somebody flings a Mattress out —
The Children hurry by —
They wonder if it died — on that —
I used to — when a Boy —

The Minister — goes stiffly in —
As if the House were His —
And He owned all the Mourners — now —
And little Boys — besides —

And then the Milliner — and the Man
Of the Appalling Trade —
To take the measure of the House —

There'll be that Dark Parade —

Of Tassels — and of Coaches — soon —
It's easy as a Sign —
The Intuition of the News —
In just a Country Town —

1862c/1896 —(J389)

Edward Dickinson was known as an austere
if not demanding man.

Later in life she dressed only in white, much to the curiosity of the town, and did so year round.

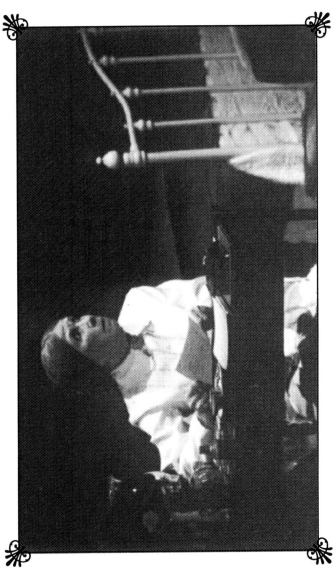

Her father rarely read her work, but she did read them to him.

To make a prairie it takes a clover and one bee,
One clover, and a bee,
And revery.
The revery alone will do,
If bees are few.

? /1896 — (J1755)

I'll tell you how the Sun rose —
A Ribbon at a time —
The Steeples swam in Amethyst —
The news, like Squirrels, ran —
The Hills untied their Bonnets —
The Bobolinks — begun —
Then I said softly to myself —
"That must have been the Sun"!
But how he set — I know not —
There seemed a purple stile
That little Yellow boys and girls
Were climbing all the while —
Till when they reached the other side,
A Dominie in Gray —
Put gently up the evening Bars —
And led the flock away —

1860c/1890 — (J318)

She had read only the Bible up until Austin began to sneak literature into the home and hide it in the piano.

"Arcturus" is his other name —
I'd rather call him "Star."
It's very mean of Science
To go and interfere!

I slew a worm the other day —
A "Savant" passing by
Murmured "Resurgam" — "Centipede"!
"Oh Lord — how frail are we"!

I pull a flower from the woods —
A monster with a glass
Computes the stamens in a breath —
And has her in a "class"!

Where as I took the Butterfly
Aforetime in my hat —
He sits erect in "Cabinets"
The Clover bells forgot.

What once was "Heaven"
Is *"Zenith"* now —
Where I proposed to go

(cont.)

Emily's reluctance to attend church did not deter
her from a strong belief in God.

When Time's brief masquerade was done
Is mapped and charted too.

What if the poles should frisk about
And stand upon their heads!
I hope I'm ready for "the worst" —
Whatever prank betides!

Perhaps the "Kingdom of Heaven's" changed -
I hope the "Children" there
Won't be "new fashioned" when I come —
And laugh at me — and stare —

I hope the Father in the skies
Will lift his little girl —
Old fashioned — naughty — everything —
Over the stile of "Pearl."

1859c/1891 — (J70)

*She preferred, as did her father, to have
Austin in Amherst.*

After law school at Harvard, Austin lived in Amherst for the remainder of his days.

Eventually, Emily stopped going to church altogether.

Some keep the Sabbath going to Church —
I keep it, staying at Home —
With a Bobolink for a Chorister —
And an Orchard, for a Dome —

Some keep the Sabbath in Surplice —
I just wear my Wings —
And instead of tolling the Bell, for Church,
Our little Sexton — sings.

God preaches, a noted Clergyman —
And the sermon is never long,
So instead of getting to Heaven, at last —
I'm going, all along.

1860c/1864 — (J324)

The Amherst and Belchertown Railroad came to Amherst in 1853 - all nineteen and a half miles of it.

I like to see it lap the Miles —
And lick the Valleys up —
And stop to feed itself at Tanks —
And then — prodigious step

Around a Pile of Mountains —
And supercilious peer
In Shanties — by the sides of Roads —
And then a Quarry pare

To fit its Ribs
And crawl between
Complaining all the while
In horrid — hooting stanza —
Then chase itself down Hill —

And neigh like Boanerges —
Then — punctual as a Star
Stop — docile and omnipotent
At its own stable door —

1862c/1891 — (J585)

*"I have a brother and sister; my mother
does not care for thought."*

I was the slightest in the House —
I took the smallest Room —
At night, my little Lamp, and Book —
And one Geranium —

So stationed I could catch the Mint
That never ceased to fall —
And just my Basket —
Let me think — I'm sure
That this was all —

I never spoke — unless addressed —
And then, 'twas brief and low —
I could not bear to live — aloud —
The Racket shamed me so —

And if it had not been so far —
And any one I knew
Were going — I had often thought
How noteless — I could die —

1862c/1945 — (J486)

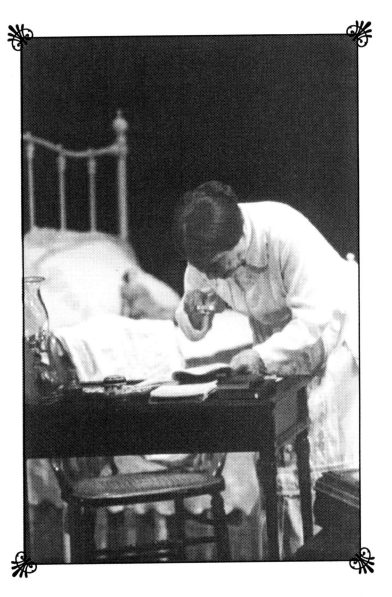

*An article in the Atlantic Monthly magazine entitled
"Letter to a Young Contributor," prompted Emily
Dickinson to send four poems.*

Her mentor became the Reverend Thomas Wentworth
Higginson of the Atlantic Monthly magazine.

At this point in her life, she had written well over 300 poems.

I taste a liquor never brewed —
From Tankards scooped in Pearl —
Not all the Vats upon the Rhine
Yield such an Alcohol!

Inebriate of Air — am I —
And Debauchee of Dew —
Reeling — thro endless summer days —
From inns of Molten Blue —

When "Landlords" turn the drunken Bee
Out of the Foxglove's door —
When Butterflies — renounce their "drams" —
I shall but drink the more!

Till Seraphs swing their snowy Hats —
And Saints — to windows run —
To see the little Tippler
Leaning against the — Sun —

1860c/1861 — (J214)

The Pedigree of Honey
Does not concern the Bee —
A Clover, any time, to him,
Is Aristocracy —

1884/1890 — (J1627)

Letters to Higginson contained other poems including,
A bird came down the walk.

A Bird came down the Walk —
He did not know I saw —
He bit an Angleworm in halves
And ate the fellow, raw,

And then he drank a Dew
From a convenient Grass —
And then hopped sidewise to the Wall
To let a Beetle pass —

He glanced with rapid eyes
That hurried all around —
They looked like frightened Beads, I thought —
He stirred his Velvet Head

Like one in danger, Cautious,
I offered him a Crumb
And he unrolled his feathers
And rowed him softer home —

Than Oars divide the Ocean,
Too silver for a seam —
Or Butterflies, off Banks of Noon
Leap, plashless as they swim.

1862c/1891 — (J328)

Of the four poems she sent: Safe in their alabaster chambers (J216), I'll tell you how the sun rose (J318), are published in this volume.

Safe in their Alabaster Chambers —
Untouched by Morning
And untouched by Noon —
Sleep the meek members of the Resurrection –
Rafter of satin,
And Roof of stone.

Light laughs the breeze
In her Castle above them —
Babbles the Bee in a stolid Ear,
Pipe the Sweet Birds in ignorant cadence —
Ah, what sagacity perished here!

(1859/1862)

Grand go the Years — in the Crescent — above
    them —
Worlds scoop their Arcs —
And Firmaments — row —
Diadems — drop — and Doges — surrender —
Soundless as dots — on a Disc of Snow —

1861/1890 — (J216)

Note: The first two stanzas are from 1859 the third is from 1861

"Forgive me if I am frightened; I never see strangers, and hardly know what I say."

When Night is almost done —
And Sunrise grows so near
That we can touch the Spaces —
It's time to smooth the Hair —

And get the Dimples ready —
And wonder we could care
For that old — faded Midnight —
That frightened — but an Hour —

1862c/1890 — (J347)

Act II

"If fame belonged to me, I could not escape her; if she
did not, the longest day would pass me on the chase."

A great Hope fell
You heard no noise
The Ruin was within
Oh cunning wreck that told no tale
And let no Witness in

The mind was built for mighty Freight
For dread occasion planned
How often foundering at Sea
Ostensibly, on Land

A not admitting of the wound
Until it grew so wide
That all my Life had entered it
And there were troughs beside

A closing of the simple lid
That opened to the sun
Until the tender Carpenter
Perpetual nail it down —

1868c/1945 — (J1123)

Emily eventually gave up on ever being a published poet.

Success is counted sweetest
By those who ne'er succeed.
To comprehend a nectar
Requires sorest need.

Not one of all the purple Host
Who took the Flag today
Can tell the definition
So clear of Victory

As he defeated — dying —
On whose forbidden ear
The distant strains of triumph
Burst agonized and clear!

1859c/1878 — (J67)

We never know how high we are
Till we are asked to rise
And then if we are true to plan
Our statures touch the skies —

The Heroism we recite
Would be a normal thing
Did not ourselves the Cubits warp
For fear to be a King —

1870c/1896 — (J1176)

*Emily was well known in town for her
baking and her garden.*

I'm Nobody! Who are you?
Are you — Nobody — Too?
Then there's a pair of us?
Don't tell! they'd advertise — you know!

How dreary — to be — Somebody!
How public — like a Frog —
To tell your name — the livelong June —
To an admiring Bog!

1861c/1891 — (J288)

Wild Nights — Wild Nights!
Were I with thee
Wild Nights should be
Our luxury!

Futile — the Winds —
To a Heart in port —
Done with the Compass —
Done with the Chart!

Rowing in Eden —
Ah, the Sea!
Might I but moor — Tonight —
In Thee!

1861c/1891 — (J249)

Emily saw Reverand Wadsworth at his Presbyterian church in Philadelphia.

Again — his voice is at the door —
I feel the old *Degree* —
I hear him ask the servant
For such an one — as me —

I take a *flower* — as I go —
My face to *justify* —
He never *saw* me — *in this life* —
I might *surprise* his eye!

I cross the Hall with *mingled* steps —
I — silent — pass the door —
I look on all this world *contains* —
Just his face — nothing more!

We talk in *careless* — and in *toss* —
A kind of *plummet* strain —
Each — sounding — shyly —
Just — how — deep —
The *other's* one — had been —

We *walk* — I leave my Dog — at home —
A *tender* — *thoughtful* Moon
Goes with us — just a little way —
And — then — we are *alone* —

(cont.)

She was so impressed by Wadsworth, it is thought that her 'Master' letters were written were to him.

Alone — if *Angels* are "alone" —
First time they *try* the *sky!*
Alone — if those "veiled faces" — be —
We cannot *count* — on High!

I'd give — to live that hour — *again* —
The *purple* — *in my Vein* —
But *He* must *count the drops* — *himself* —
My price for *every stain!*

1862c/1945 — (J663)

If Wadsworth was her Master, then his visit becomes even more defining.

I cannot live with You —
It would be Life —
And Life is over there —
Behind the Shelf

The Sexton keeps the Key to —
Putting up
Our Life — His Porcelain
Like a Cup —

Discarded of the Housewife —
Quaint — or Broke —
A newer Sevres pleases —
Old Ones crack —

I could not die — with You —
For One must wait
To shut the Other's Gaze down —
You — could not —

And I — Could I stand by
And see You — freeze —
Without my Right of Frost —
Death's privilege?

Nor could I rise — with You —
Because Your Face
Would put out Jesus' —
That New Grace

(cont.)

The answer to the mystery of Emily's writings of romance eludes everyone.

Glow plain — and foreign
On my homesick Eye —
Except that You than He
Shone closer by —

They'd judge Us — How —
For You — served Heaven —You know,
Or sought to —
I could not —

Because You saturated Sight —
And I had no more Eyes
For sordid excellence
As Paradise

And were You lost, I would be —
Though My Name
Rang loudest
On the Heavenly fame —

And were You — saved —
And I — condemned to be
Where You were not —
That self — were Hell to Me —

So We must meet apart —
You there — I here —
With just the Door ajar
That Oceans are — and Prayer —
And that White Sustenance —
Despair —

1862c/1890 — (J640)

It was their last time together - he died in 1883.

Will there really be a "Morning"?
Is there such a thing as "Day"?
Could I see it from the mountains
If I were as tall as they?

Has it feet like Water lilies?
Has it feathers like a Bird?
Is it brought from famous countries
Of which I have never heard?

Oh some Scholar! Oh some Sailor!
Oh some Wise Man from the skies!
Please to tell a little Pilgrim
Where the place called "Morning" lies!

1859c/1891 — (J101)

*Samuel Bowles, Editor of <u>The Springfield Republican</u>,
published this poem in 1866.*

A narrow Fellow in the Grass
Occasionally rides —
You may have met Him — did you not
His notice sudden is —

The Grass divides as with a Comb —
A spotted shaft is seen —
And then it closes at your feet
And opens further on —

He likes a Boggy Acre
A Floor too cool for Corn —
Yet when a Boy, and Barefoot —
I more than once at Noon
Have passed, I thought, a Whip lash
Unbraiding in the Sun
When stooping to secure it
It wrinkled, and was gone —

Several of Nature's People
I know, and they know me —
I feel for them a transport
Of cordiality —

But never met this Fellow
Attended, or alone
Without a tighter breathing
And Zero at the Bone —

1865c/1866 — (J986)

*On a trip to Boston, in June of 1874, Emily's
father Edward died of a heart attack.*

My life closed twice before its close —
It yet remains to see
If Immortality unveil
A third event to me

So huge, so hopeless to conceive
As these that twice befell.
Parting is all we know of heaven,
And all we need of hell.

? /1896 — (J1732)

She died — *this* was the way she died.
And when her breath was done
Took up her simple wardrobe
And started for the sun.
Her little figure at the gate
The Angels must have spied,
Since I could never find her
Upon the mortal side.

1859c/1891 — (J150)

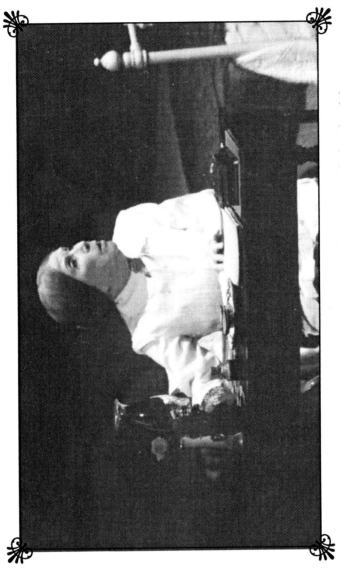

Her mother's long illness would continue to erode her health.
Emily and Lavinia took constant care of her.

"Hope" is the thing with feathers —
That perches in the soul —
And sings the tune without the words —
And never stops — at all —

And sweetest — in the Gale — is heard —
And sore must be the storm —
That could abash the little Bird
That kept so many warm —

I've heard it in the chillest land —
And on the strangest Sea —
Yet, never, in Extremity,
It asked a crumb — of Me.

186c1/1891 — (J254)

Emily, though she never left her father's house for the last twenty years of her life, traveled through her mind.

I never saw a Moor —
I never saw the Sea —
Yet know I how the Heather looks
And what a Billow be

I never spoke with God
Nor visited in Heaven —
Yet certain am I of the spot
As if the Checks were given —

1865c/1890 — (J1052)

*Nothing else in Emily's life saddened her more than
little Gilbert's passing.*

I tie my Hat — I crease my Shawl —
Life's little duties do — precisely —
As the very least
Were infinite — to me —

I put new Blossoms in the Glass
And throw the old — away —
I push a petal from my Gown
That anchored there — I weigh
The time 'twill be till six o'clock
I have so much to do —
And yet — Existence — some way back —
Stopped — struck — My ticking — through —
We cannot put Ourself away
As a completed Man
Or Woman — When the Errand's done
We came to Flesh — upon —
There may be — Miles on Miles of Nought —
Of Action — sicker far —
To simulate — is stinging work —
To cover what we are
From Science — and from Surgery
Too Telescopic Eyes
To bear on us unshaded —
For their — sake — not for Ours —

(cont.)

*In her last year of good health, Emily and her younger
sister Lavinia lived alone at The Homestead, caring for
each other.*

'Twould start them —
We — could tremble —
But since we got a Bomb —
And held it in our Bosom —
Nay — Hold it — it is calm —

Therefore — we do life's labor —
Though life's Reward — be done —
With scrupulous exactness —
To hold our Senses — on —

1862c/1929 — (J443)

I reason, Earth is short —
And Anguish — absolute —
And many hurt,
But, what of that?

I reason, we could die —
The best Vitality
Cannot excel Decay,
But, what of that?

I reason, that in Heaven —
Somehow, it will be even —
Some new Equation, given —
But, what of that?

1862c/1890 — (J301)

Emily had her first attack of Bright's disease. It would debilitate her and after two years, take her life.

Of all the Sounds despatched abroad,
There's not a Charge to me
Like that old measure in the Boughs —
That phraseless Melody —
The Wind does — working like a Hand,
Whose fingers Comb the Sky —
Then quiver down — with tufts of Tune —
Permitted Gods, and me —

Inheritance, it is, to us —
Beyond the Art to Earn —
Beyond the trait to take away
By Robber, since the Gain
Is gotten not of fingers —
And inner than the Bone —
Hid golden, for the whole of Days,
And even in the Urn,
I cannot vouch the merry Dust
Do not arise and play
In some odd fashion of its own,
Some quainter Holiday,
When Winds go round and round in Bands —
And thrum upon the door,
And Birds take places, overhead,
To bear them Orchestra.

I crave Him grace of Summer Boughs,
If such an Outcast be —

(cont.)

*Emily had wanted a service in her own home, and to
be carried through the garden to the cemetery.*

Who never heard that fleshless Chant —
Rise — solemn — on the Tree,
As if some Caravan of Sound
Off Deserts, in the Sky,
Had parted Rank,
Then knit, and swept —
In Seamless Company —

1862c/1890 — (J321)

In spite of her illness, she still wrote poetry –
eleven in 1885 with her last year bringing two.

I'm ceded — I've stopped being Theirs —
The name They dropped upon my face
With water, in the country church
Is finished using, now,
And They can put it with my Dolls.
My childhood, and the string of spools,
I've finished threading — too —

Baptized, before, without the choice,
But this time, consciously, of Grace —
Unto supremest name —
Called to my Full - The Crescent dropped —
Existence's whole Arc, filled up,
With one small Diadem.

My second Rank — too small the first —
Crowned — Crowing — on my Father's breast –
A half unconscious Queen —
By this time — Adequate — Erect,
With Will to choose, or to reject,
And I choose, just a Crown —

1862c/1890 — (J508)

Shortly before Emily died, she sent a note to her cousins.
It read: "Called back." Emily somehow, seemed to know.

Because I could not stop for Death —
He kindly stopped for me —
The Carriage held but just Ourselves —
And Immortality.

We slowly drove — He knew no haste
And I had put away
My labor and my leisure too,
For his Civility —

We passed the School, where Children strove
At Recess — in the Ring —
We passed the Fields of Gazing Grain —
We passed the Setting Sun —

Or rather - He passed Us —
The Dews drew quivering and chill —
For only Gossamer, my Gown -
My Tippet — only Tulle —

We paused before a House that seemed
A Swelling of the Ground —
The Roof was scarcely visible —
The Cornice — in the Ground —

Since then — 'tis Centuries — and yet
Feels shorter than the Day
I first surmised the Horses' Heads
Were toward Eternity —

1863c/1890 — (J712)

*After Emily's death, Lavinia found 60 packets
containing some 900 poems in a box.*

This is my letter to the World
That never wrote to Me —
The simple news that Nature told —
With tender Majesty

Her Message is committed
To Hands I cannot see —
For love of Her — Sweet — countrymen —
Judge tenderly — of Me

1862c/1890 — (J441)

It's all I have to bring today —
This, and my heart beside —
This, and my heart, and all the fields —
And all the meadows wide —
Be sure you count — should I forget
Some one the sum could tell —
This, and my heart, and all the Bees
Which in the Clover dwell.

1858c/1896 — (J26)

The End

List of First Lines

Poem   **Page**

A Bird came down the Walk 71
A great Hope fell 79
A narrow Fellow in the Grass 95
A word is dead 39
Again - his voice is at the door.. 85
"Arcturus" is his other name 55
Awake ye muses nine, sing me a strain divine................. 41
Because I could not stop for Death................................. 113
"Hope" is the thing with feathers 99
I cannot live with You 89
I dwell in Possibility.. 45
I like to see it lap the Miles 63
I never saw a Moor.. 101
I reason, Earth is short 105
I tie my Hat - I crease my Shawl 103
I taste a liquor never brewed 69
I was the slightest in the House 65
I'll tell you how the Sun rose 53
I'm Nobody! Who are you? 83
I'm ceded - I've stopped being Theirs 111
If I can stop one Heart from breaking 39
It's all I have to bring today 115
My life closed twice before its close 97
Of all the Sounds despatched abroad 107
Safe in their Alabaster Chambers - (& 1861/1890) 73
She died - this was the way she died 97
Some keep the Sabbath going to Church 61
Success is counted sweetest... 81
Surgeons must be very careful 37
Tell all the Truth but tell it slant 37
The Pedigree of Honey 69
The Soul selects her own Society 33
There's been a Death, in the Opposite House 49
This Me - that walks and works - must die 45
This is my letter to the World 115
To make a prairie it takes a clover and one bee 53
We never know how high we are 81
When Night is almost done 75
Wild Nights - Wild Nights! 83
Will there really be a "Morning"? 93

Bibliography

The Complete Poems of Emily Dickinson, 1955
> Edited by Thomas H. Johnson
> Published by Little, Brown and Company, Boston

Emily Dickinson's Home, 1955
> By Millicent Todd Bingham
> Published by Harper & Brothers Publishers, New York

The Belle of Amherst, 1978
> A Play by William Luce
> Published by Houghton Mifflin Company, Boston

Readings on Emily Dickinson, 1997
> Edited by Bruno Leone, Scott Barbour,
>   Bonnie Szumski and Tamara Johnson
> Published by Greenhaven Press, San Diego

Emily Dickinson and Her Contemporaries, 1998
> By Elizabeth A. Petrino
> Published by University Press of New England

The Emily Dickinson Handbook, 1998
> Edited by Gudrun Grabher, Roland Hagenbüchle
>   and Christanne Miller
> Published by University of Massachusetts Press, Amherst

Colophon

This book is published by
The Paragon Agency
P.O. Box 1281 • Orange, California • 92856
(714) 771-0652
www.SpecialBooks.com

This book is made with White Opaque Book stock
and is set in Century Expanded,
a typeface first commissioned in 1894.

The style and layout differ from old standards in publication and elements such as dates. All punctuation is within parentheses and quotes; commas do not precede the words: *or – and – but* or *although*; year dates are suffixed as *1880s* and *1882c* in reference to a range of years and circa, respectively.

The author wishes to acknowledge the assistance of
The Laguna Playhouse
in the production of this book.

This commemorates the 25th Anniversary
of the play
The Belle of Amherst.